ROD CAREW
SECOND BASEMAN

MINNESOTA
TWINS

BOB ALLISON
LEFT FIELDER

MINNESOTA
TWINS

THE STORY OF THE MINNESOTA TWINS

Published by Creative Education
P.O. Box 227, Mankato, Minnesota 56002
Creative Education is an imprint of The Creative Company
www.thecreativecompany.us

Design and production by Blue Design
Art direction by Rita Marshall
Printed by Corporate Graphics in the United States of America

Photographs by AP Images (Elise Amendola), Corbis (Bettmann, Minnesota Historical Society, Brian Snyder/Reuters), Getty Images (Diamond Images, Stephen Dunn, Focus on Sport, Judy Griesedieck/Time & Life Pictures, Leon Halip, Bruce Kluckhohn, Richard Mackson/Sports Illustrated, Jim McIsaac, Ronald C. Modra/Sports Imagery, National Baseball Hall of Fame Library/MLB Photos, Tom Pigeon/Allsport, Rich Pilling/MLB Photos, Bill Polo/MLB Photos, Louis Reqeuna/MLB Photos, Joe Robbins, Herb Scharfman/ Sports Imagery, Jon SooHoo/MLB Photos, Tony Tomsic/MLB Photos, Tim Umphrey, Alex Wong)

Library of Congress Cataloging-in-Publication Data

LeBoutillier, Nate.
The story of the Minnesota Twins / by Nate LeBoutillier.
p. cm. — (Baseball: the great American game)
Includes index.
Summary: The history of the Minnesota Twins professional baseball team from its inaugural 1901 season as the Washington Senators to today, spotlighting the team's greatest players and most memorable moments.
ISBN 978-1-60818-047-9
1. Minnesota Twins (Baseball team)—History—Juvenile literature. I. Title. II. Title: Minnesota Twins. III. Series.

GV875.M55L43 2011
796.357'6409776579—dc22   2010025204

CPSIA: 110310 PO1381

First Edition
9 8 7 6 5 4 3 2 1

Page 3: Right fielder Tony Oliva
Page 4: First baseman Justin Morneau

BASEBALL: THE GREAT AMERICAN GAME

THE STORY OF THE MINNESOTA TWINS

Nate LeBoutillier

CREATIVE EDUCATION

CONTENTS

BALL UP NORTH

The "Twin Cities" of Minneapolis and St. Paul would be one city but for the mighty Mississippi River that divides them. That dividing line does, however, mark a difference in style as well as city limits. Minneapolis is modern and ever-changing, while St. Paul is older and more mature. Even the local architecture helps define the cities' contrasting personalities, as Minneapolis's buildings tend to be sleek and sided by an abundance of glass, while St. Paul's are often block-shaped and stony.

One thing the Twin Cities have always had in common, though, is a passion for baseball. Local teams named the Minneapolis Millers and St. Paul Saints emerged way back in the 1870s. In 1961, Major League Baseball finally made its way to Minnesota when a team founded in 1901 in Washington, D.C., and known as the Senators was relocated to the Twin Cities and renamed the Minnesota Twins.

The Senators-turned-Twins came to the Midwest with a story that revolved largely around one of the greatest pitchers in baseball history. Walter Johnson, a sidearming right-hander, led the American League

With its framed view of the Minneapolis skyline, Target Field earned accolades as one of baseball's most beautiful parks when it opened in 2010.

PITCHER · BERT BLYLEVEN

A reliable starter with a baffling curveball, Blyleven played 22 major-league seasons and won 287 games. Ten and a half of those seasons and 149 of those wins were with Minnesota. A man with a great sense of humor, Blyleven could both take it and dish it out. Teammates who would tease him about the high number of home runs he gave up (he led the major leagues in 1986 and 1987) might find themselves with a whipped cream pie in their face during a TV interview, courtesy of Blyleven. Since 1995, he has worked as a color commentator on Twins television broadcasts.

STATS

BERT BLYLEVEN
PITCHER

MINNESOTA
TWINS

Twins seasons: 1970–76, 1985–88

Height: 6-foot-3

Weight: 205

- **60 career complete-game shutouts**

- **3,701 career strikeouts**

- **2-time All-Star**

- **Baseball Hall of Fame inductee (2011)**

(AL) in strikeouts for eight straight seasons, from 1912 to 1919, and set many other records during a long and fruitful pitching career. In 1924, as a 36-year-old veteran, "The Big Train" rang up a 23–7 record with 158 strikeouts to lead the Senators all the way to their first World Series championship. The next season, Washington was upended in the "Fall Classic" by the Pittsburgh Pirates, and in 1933, the club again finished runner-up, this time to the New York Giants.

The Senators were plagued by disappointing play in the decades that followed until, in 1961, team owner Calvin Griffith decided to give the franchise a fresh start—and name—in Minnesota. Among the Twins' first young stars were infielder/outfielder Harmon Killebrew, a home run hitter extraordinaire; right fielder Tony Oliva, who would win the 1964 AL Rookie of the Year award; scrappy outfielder Bob Allison; and hard-hitting shortstop Zoilo Versalles. On the mound, Minnesota

TONY OLIVA

featured Jim "Mudcat" Grant and Jim Kaat, who would become the all-time winningest pitcher in Twins history.

Minnesota finished a close second to the New York Yankees in the race for the AL pennant in both 1962 and 1963. Then, in 1965, the Twins went 102–60 to win the pennant and earn the right to face the Los Angeles Dodgers in the World Series. The teams played the first six games of the series to a draw, but in Game 7, ace pitcher Sandy Koufax shut out Minnesota 2–0 to give Los Angeles the championship. "You hate to lose, but we didn't disgrace ourselves," said Twins manager Sam Mele. "We were beaten by the best pitcher that there is anywhere."

Despite the loss, Minnesota fans were confident that their slugging Twins would get another shot at the title and came in league-leading droves to Metropolitan Stadium. However, the 1966 Twins finished a distant second to the loaded Baltimore Orioles, who went on to defeat the Dodgers in the World Series. The Twins bolstered their lineup even further in 1967 with the addition of rookie second baseman Rod Carew, whose superb batting eye helped him win the AL Rookie of the Year award. "Rod Carew could get more hits with a soup bone than I could get with a rack full of bats," said Twins outfielder Steve Brye.

ROD CAREW

Rod Carew proved that exceptional hitting doesn't necessarily require power, winning the 1972 batting title without hitting a single home run. He was so valuable to the Twins and, later, the California Angels that both clubs retired his number.

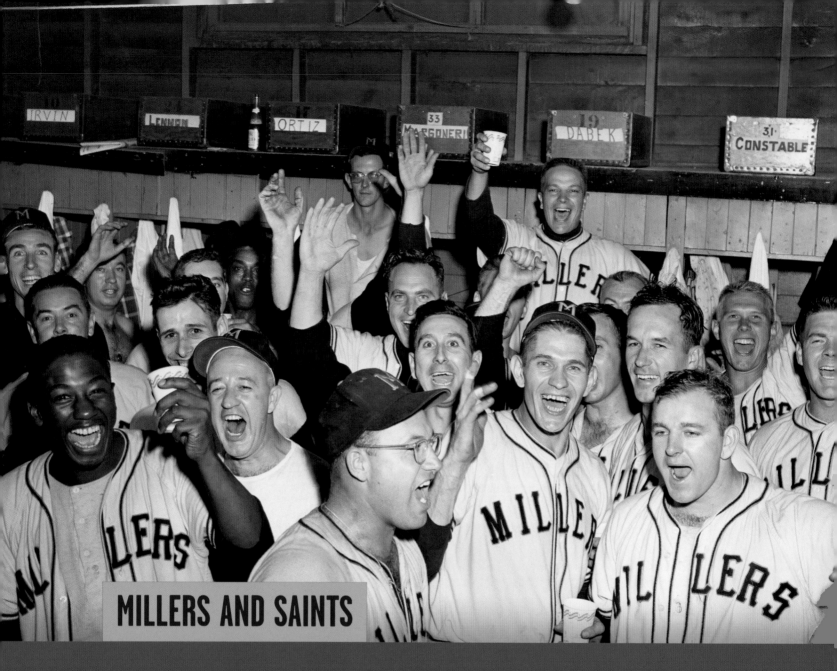

MILLERS AND SAINTS

Baseball history is rich in Minnesota, dating back to the post-Civil War baseball boom of the 1870s. By 1884, the Northwestern League contained many teams, two of which were located in Minneapolis and St. Paul. The Western League—which would later become the present-day American League—was founded in the 1890s, and it featured the Minneapolis Millers and St. Paul Saints. In 1902, the Saints and Millers became charter members of the American Association, a minor league that would feature the two teams until the Minnesota Twins came to town in 1961. The Millers and Saints played 22 intercity

games each summer, and on the holidays of Decoration Day, the Fourth of July, and Labor Day, a doubleheader would be played that included a morning game in either Lexington Park in St. Paul or Nicollet Park in Minneapolis, a streetcar ride across the mighty Mississippi River, and then an afternoon game in the opposite ballpark. Many legendary players competed for the Millers and Saints on their way to the major leagues, including Ted Williams, Willie Mays, Duke Snider, and Roy Campanella. In all, 23 players now enshrined in the Baseball Hall of Fame once played for either the Millers or the Saints.

CATCHER · JOE MAUER

Built more like a football quarterback than a traditionally squat-framed catcher, Joe Mauer, when crouching, nearly topped some of the league's shorter batsmen in height. Mauer grew up in St. Paul, Minnesota, rooting for the Twins as a boy, and the club nabbed him with the first overall pick of baseball's 2001 amateur draft. The catcher soon rose from the minors to the majors and emerged as one of baseball's greatest all-around stars. In 2009, after missing the season's entire first month with an injury, Mauer hit a homer in his first at bat and never let up from there, winning the AL Most Valuable Player (MVP) award.

JOE MAUER
CATCHER

MINNESOTA
TWINS

STATS

Twins seasons: 2004–present

Height: 6-foot-5

Weight: 220

- **.327 career BA**

- **3-time AL leader in BA**

- **3-time Gold Glove winner**

- **2009 AL MVP**

FIRST BASEMAN · KENT HRBEK

A homegrown standout, this Bloomington, Minnesota, native was a solid fixture at first base for the Twins for more than a decade. In his first game in a Twins uniform, Hrbek hit a game-winning homer in the 12th inning. The 1982 All-Star and runner-up for AL Rookie of the Year was also an avid outdoorsman, hunting and fishing when his baseball schedule permitted.

KENT HRBEK
FIRST BASEMAN

MINNESOTA
TWINS

Hrbek played a big role in boosting the Twins to World Series titles in 1987 and 1991, with a key highlight being a Game 6 grand slam against the St. Louis Cardinals in 1987 that helped win the game, 11–5.

STATS

Twins seasons: 1981–94

Height: 6-foot-4

Weight: 260

- .282 career BA

- 293 career HR

- 1,086 career RBI

- Uniform number (14) retired by Twins

The Twins went 91–71 in 1967, but the Boston Red Sox squeaked past them by a single game to take the pennant. The team was a disappointment in 1968, but the same core of players that nearly won the 1965 World Series remained confident that a championship was within reach. Major League Baseball decided to split the American and National Leagues into two divisions apiece in 1969, and Minnesota landed in the AL Western Division.

INTO THE DOME

ew pitcher Dave Boswell and holdover Jim Perry each won 20 games for the Twins in 1969, and outfielder Cesar Tovar teamed up with Carew, Oliva, and the 1969 AL MVP Killebrew to pace a formidable offense. But despite winning the AL West in both 1969 and 1970, the Twins continued to be thwarted by Baltimore, getting swept in the playoffs by the Orioles both times. "We had some great ballclubs back then," Killebrew later said, "but Baltimore always had our number."

The 1970 season was Minnesota's last hurrah for a while, and the

Twins hovered near the .500 mark throughout the 1970s, turning in solid but unspectacular performances. Fans bid farewell to several longtime heroes as Killebrew's career wound down and Oliva succumbed to knee problems. Seventeen seasons would pass after the Twins' postseason battles with Baltimore before Minnesota fans would experience playoff excitement again.

Carew won the AL MVP award in 1977, and pitcher Bert Blyleven threw a curveball that bent crazily, baffling many an opposing batter in the '70s. But owner Calvin Griffith, saddled with financial problems, then replaced the majority of the club's highly paid veterans—including Carew and Blyleven—with younger, less expensive players. The Twins celebrated 20 years of big-league baseball in Minnesota in 1981 by finishing dead last in the AL West, and fan attendance at Met Stadium dropped to new lows. Second baseman John Castino led all Twins hitters in 1981 with a paltry .268 batting average, shortstop Roy Smalley was the team's top home run hitter with just seven dingers, and the most wins a Twins pitcher could muster was nine, recorded by Pete Redfern.

JOHN CASTINO

Although he came to symbolize a bleak period in Twins history in the eyes of some fans, infielder John Castino gave Minnesota some quality performances, posting a .302 batting average in 1980 and leading the AL with nine triples in 1981.

SECOND BASEMAN · ROD CAREW

With a quick bat and lightning speed on the base paths, Carew burst upon the major-league scene in 1967, batting .292 and winning Rookie of the Year honors. Never much of a power hitter, Carew was content to cock his bat back only halfway and flick it rather than really swing it, which let him slap the ball to all parts of the field and use his lively legs. Carew was most famous for stealing home plate seven times in 1969, a major-league record. Although Carew's 3,000th career hit came as a member of the California Angels, he got it against, fittingly, the Twins.

STATS

Twins seasons: 1967–78

Height: 6 feet

Weight: 180

- .328 career BA

- 18-time All-Star

- 1977 AL MVP

- Baseball Hall of Fame inductee (1991)

ROD CAREW
SECOND BASEMAN

MINNESOTA
TWINS

The Twins set franchise records for futility in 1982 with a 14-game losing streak and a 60–102 final mark, but that season represented a changing of the guard. The team moved into the Hubert H. Humphrey Metrodome—an indoor stadium with a Teflon roof that looked like a big bubble—in downtown Minneapolis, and new heroes emerged.

Rookie first baseman Kent Hrbek, a Minnesota boy as big as a bear yet quick as a cat, batted .301 in 1982 and was named an All-Star. Hard-hitting Gary Gaetti played third base with high energy and a sure glove, and right fielder Tom Brunansky wielded a booming bat. Joining the pitching staff was crafty left-hander Frank Viola. Although the Twins floundered again in 1982, something was building.

In 1982, the Twins also drafted a round, 5-foot-9 third baseman named Kirby Puckett. Puckett broke into the Twins' starting lineup as an outfielder in 1984, and his nonstop hustle and ever-present smile quickly endeared him to fans. "Scouts would always tell me I was too short, or too heavy, or too whatever," said Puckett, who would remain in center field throughout his career. "But baseball isn't about being a shape or a size. It's about how big you are inside that counts."

DOME-FIELD ADVANTAGE

From raised to lowered pitching mounds, eccentric outfield walls, or peculiar foul territories, major league baseball teams have always sought a home-field advantage. When the Twins began playing their home games in the Hubert H. Humphrey Metrodome in Minneapolis in 1982, becoming just the third team to play under an artificial sky (after the Houston Astros and Seattle Mariners), they acquired a ballpark full of quirks. Opposing players often complained of losing track of fly balls due to the baseball-colored roof, batted balls would skip and bounce off the artificial turf as if they were toy superballs, and, occasionally, high popups would deflect off hanging speakers (which were deemed "in play") or even the rooftop itself. In 2003, Dick Ericson, a Dome groundskeeper from 1982 to 1995, made news when he admitted that he sometimes turned the stadium's air conditioning on and off during games in the hopes of affecting the flight of baseballs to the Twins' advantage. "I became very suspicious, maybe paranoid," said Bobby Valentine, former manager of the Texas Rangers. "They had such an uncanny way of winning." In 2010, the team left the Metrodome and its quirky benefits behind as it moved across downtown Minneapolis into the new Target Field.

THE METRODOME

In 1986, Puckett helped give Minnesota a powerful offense. Unfortunately, the team's pitching was weak, and the Twins sank low in the standings again with a 71–91 record. Late in that season, however, Minnesota made a pivotal move, hiring 36-year-old Tom Kelly as the youngest manager in the majors. Under Kelly's stoic guidance, the Twins quickly improved.

THE TWIN TITLES

iola and veteran Bert Blyleven (back in a Minnesota uniform for a second stint) headed up the Twins' pitching crew in 1987, combining for 32 wins, and closer Jeff Reardon racked up 31 saves. Meanwhile, Hrbek, Puckett, Gaetti, and Brunansky each slugged at least 28 homers as the upstart Twins won the 1987 AL West crown with an 85–77 record. "We just do what T.K. [Kelly] tells us," Puckett explained. "Don't get too high, don't get too low. Just go out, give 100 percent, and we'll win the battle one game at a time."

In the 1987 AL Championship Series (ALCS), the Twins toppled the team with the best record in the majors, the Detroit Tigers, four games

THIRD BASEMAN · HARMON KILLEBREW

At age 18, Killebrew was the youngest player in the major leagues when he broke into the Washington Senators' lineup in 1954. "The Killer" never once topped .300 in his 14 seasons of service in Minnesota, but hitting for average wasn't Killebrew's game—hitting the long ball was. In 1967, he slugged the longest home run (520 feet) in Twins history. Killebrew walloped the homer into the sixth row of the upper deck of Metropolitan Stadium, cracking the seat, which was later painted a commemorative orange. He holds many of the Twins' franchise records for longevity, including games played (1,939).

HARMON KILLEBREW
THIRD BASEMAN

MINNESOTA
TWINS

STATS

Senators/Twins seasons: 1954–74

Height: 5-foot-11

Weight: 215

- 573 career HR

- 1,584 career RBI

- 1969 AL MVP

- Baseball Hall of Fame inductee (1984)

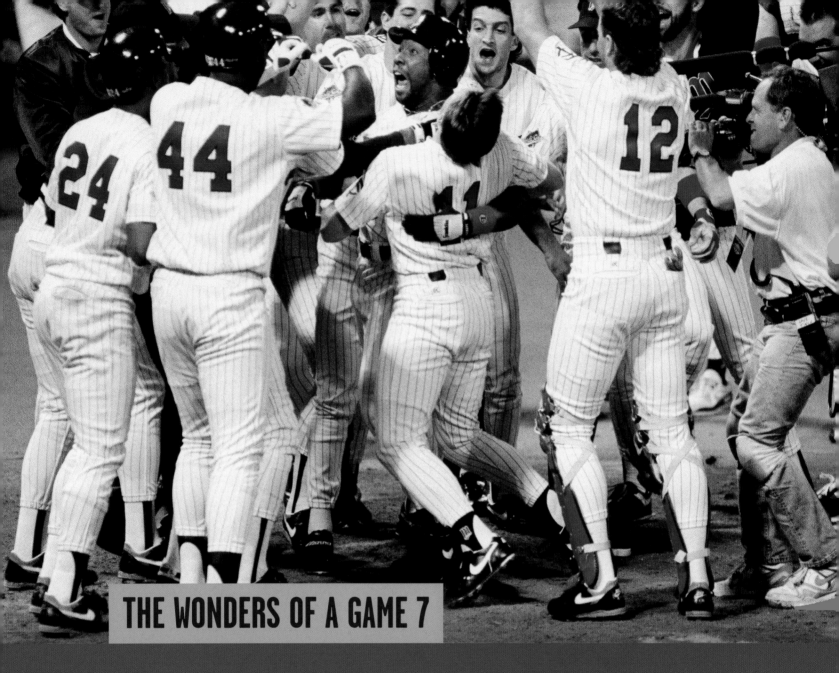

THE WONDERS OF A GAME 7

There's nothing like the drama of playing in a Game 7 for a championship. The Twins have been fortunate enough to have been involved in three World Series Game 7s. The 1965 Game 7 featured two dominant southpaw pitchers, Minnesota's Jim Kaat and the Los Angeles Dodgers' legendary ace, Sandy Koufax. Fighting chronic arm pain, Koufax started Game 7 on just two days' rest yet pitched a three-hit shutout in the Dodgers' 2–0 win. In 1987's Game 7, the Twins relied on their "10th man"—the screaming, handkerchief-waving Metrodome crowd—and the pitching of Frank Viola to earn a 4–2 win over the St. Louis Cardinals. Jack Morris was the hero in the Twins' 1991 Game 7 victory, pitching 10 shutout innings to best Atlanta Braves pitcher John Smoltz, who pitched a scoreless 9 innings only to watch the Twins win in the bottom of the 10th, when they scored the game's lone run. "You feel so numb that you could go in for surgery and not need any anesthetic," said Twins outfielder Tom Brunansky in 1987 after the thrilling Game 7 win. "The sprint to the pile, the jumping on everybody—you don't feel your feet touching the ground."

to one. For the first time in 22 years, the Twins were going to the World Series. Just as in 1965, the Twins of 1987 were considered underdogs—this time to St. Louis's mighty Cardinals. But the Twins surprised the experts by crushing the Cardinals 10–1 and 8–4 in front of ear-splitting Metrodome crowds in the first two games.

St. Louis won the next three games in a row at their home ballpark, Busch Stadium, taking the series lead back to "the Dome." Minnesota's offense roared in an 11–5 Game 6 win, setting up a dramatic Game 7. Viola took the mound for the Twins and lived up to his nickname of "Sweet Music," fooling Cardinals hitters with his masterful "circle changeup" pitch and surrendering only six hits as the Twins won 4–2 to take home the World Series championship trophy. "We're no longer the Twinkies," said Twins second baseman Steve Lombardozzi, referring to critics who—during Minnesota's losing years—nicknamed the Twins after the soft, cream-filled confection. "We are the world champion Minnesota Twins."

The Twins could not repeat the feat the following season, and by 1990, they had stumbled back into last place with a 74–88 record. Blyleven and

Viola had been traded away, and Minnesota's young pitchers struggled. "We just aren't getting it done on the mound," said Kelly. "But hopefully the lumps we take now will pay off down the road."

Minnesota sputtered early in 1991 but caught fire in June, winning a franchise-record 15 straight games. Pitcher Scott Erickson topped the AL with 20 wins on the season, leading a rebuilt pitching staff that featured Kevin Tapani, veteran Jack Morris, and reliever Rick Aguilera. A key addition to the offense was hustling second baseman Chuck Knoblauch, who captured the 1991 AL Rookie of the Year award.

The Twins finished atop their division with a 95–67 mark and trounced the Toronto Blue Jays in the ALCS, four games to one. Just as in 1987, the 1991 Twins had gone from worst to first in their division and fought their way to the World Series. This time they met the Atlanta Braves, another "Cinderella" team that had also finished in last place in its division the previous season.

The 1991 World Series played out in epic fashion, going seven nail-biting games—five of which were decided by a single run. As in 1987, the Twins won the first two games in the Metrodome but lost the next three on the road. With Minnesota facing elimination, Puckett dominated Game 6, making a spectacular leaping catch in the third inning and knocking an

KIRBY PUCKETT

SHORTSTOP · ZOILO VERSALLES

Zoilo Versalles, a Cuban-born speedster, was a blur on the baseball diamond, whether using his quick reaction time to showcase expansive fielding range from the shortstop position or zipping around the base paths to score lots of runs. As the Twins' leadoff batter in the '60s, Versalles set the table for such power-hitting teammates as Harmon Killebrew, Bob Allison, and Tony Oliva. In 1965, the free-swinging Versalles led the AL in doubles, triples, runs scored—and strikeouts. His superb 1965 season made him the first player in Twins history to win the AL MVP award and helped power Minnesota to its first World Series.

ZOILO VERSALLES
SHORTSTOP

MINNESOTA
TWINS

STATS

Senators/Twins seasons: 1959–67

Height: 5-foot-10

Weight: 150

• 2-time Gold Glove winner

• 3-time AL leader in triples

• 2-time All-Star

• 1965 AL MVP

JACK MORRIS

11th-inning pitch into the left-field stands to win the game and extend the series.

Game 7 pitted Morris, a St. Paul native, against Braves ace John Smoltz. Each was outstanding, and the game remained scoreless after nine innings. Kelly told Morris he intended to bring in a reliever in the 10th, but the hot-tempered hurler insisted on returning to the mound. "I would have needed a shotgun to get him out of the game," said Kelly. "And I didn't have one."

Morris pitched a clean 10th inning, and it would be all the Twins would need. In the bottom of the 10th, Minnesota loaded the bases, and then pinch hitter Gene Larkin looped a hit into left field. The Metrodome crowd let loose a frenzied roar as outfielder Dan Gladden leaped onto home plate to give Minnesota its second world title. Fay Vincent, the commissioner of baseball, said it best when he noted, "It was probably the greatest World Series ever."

Minnesota's reign atop the baseball world ended the next season when the Twins missed the playoffs. In 1993, the Twins went a disappointing 71–91, the first of what would be eight straight losing seasons. Team owner Carl Pohlad (who had purchased the franchise

LEFT FIELDER · BOB ALLISON

In his first full major-league season with the Washington Senators in 1959, Allison was voted both Rookie of the Year and an All-Star. He went on to make the All-Star team two more times (in 1963 and 1964) after the franchise moved to Minnesota. As a fixture in left field for the highly successful Twins of the 1960s, Allison is probably best remembered for a single play he made in Game 2 of the 1965 World Series—a run-saving, backhanded, diving catch. In college, the hard-nosed yet versatile Allison played fullback for the University of Kansas football team.

STATS

Senators/Twins seasons: 1958–70

Height: 6-foot-4

Weight: 220

• 256 career HR

• 796 career RBI

• 1959 AL leader in triples (9)

• 3-time All-Star

BOB ALLISON
LEFT FIELDER

MINNESOTA
TWINS

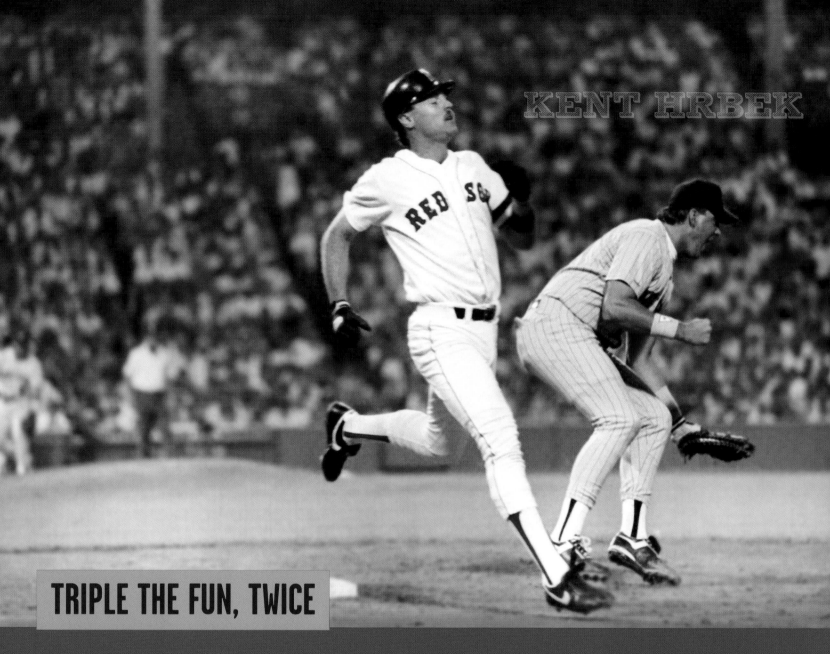

KENT HRBEK

TRIPLE THE FUN, TWICE

The triple play is one of baseball's rarest events—in more than 100 years of big-league baseball, the average number of triple plays turned is approximately 5 per season—and since the Twins started playing in Minnesota in 1961, the team has turned just 10. But on July 17, 1990, at Boston's legendary Fenway Park in a game versus the Red Sox, the Twins turned not one but two triple plays in the same game—a feat never before accomplished in the majors. The first triple play occurred in the fourth inning, when former Twins outfielder Tom Brunansky came to bat for the Red Sox with men on first and second. Brunansky hit a sharp grounder to Twins third baseman Gary Gaetti, who stepped on third and threw to second baseman Al Newman for the force out. Newman in turn wheeled and fired to first baseman Kent Hrbek in time to force out Brunansky. In the eighth inning, the Twins turned three in the exact same fashion—Gaetti to Newman to Hrbek—when Red Sox second baseman Jodi Reed hit a rocket to third. Despite those two history-making plays, the Twins lost the game, 1–0.

DAN GLADDEN

from Griffith in 1984) cut the club's payroll dramatically, and the organization's pool of talent in the minor leagues was frightfully shallow.

In 1995, power-hitting left fielder Marty Cordova slugged his way to the AL Rookie of the Year award. Brad Radke, a control pitcher, also performed admirably, but the losses continued to mount. Then, in spring training before the 1996 season, longtime star Kirby Puckett developed blurred vision in his right eye—a disease called glaucoma— and was forced to retire. Five years after standing atop the baseball world, the Twins were at the bottom.

CONTENDERS AGAIN

n the mid-1990s, the Twins were led by several veterans in the twilight of bright careers who returned to spend their final big-league seasons in their native state of Minnesota. These included infielder Paul Molitor, designated hitter Dave Winfield, and catcher Terry Steinbach. Although the Twins continued to lose many games, the players and fans appreciated Kelly's approach to coaching. "He concentrates on playing the game right," said Steinbach. "His players run balls out. They hit the cutoff man. They don't showboat or hot dog."

Pohlad slashed the Twins' payroll to a league-low $15 million in 1998, leaving the team with a lineup full of inexperienced youngsters. Then, just when it seemed the Twins were beyond hope, the outlook brightened. In 2001, Puckett and Winfield were inducted into the Baseball Hall of Fame, and the Twins made some shrewd drafts and trades to bulk up their minor-league prospects. As the team moved into a new century, general manager Terry Ryan built up a low-cost club with potential.

The scrappy Twins led the AL Central Division (which had been formed in 1994) for much of the 2001 season before finishing second to the Cleveland Indians with an 85–77 record. But Major League Baseball then unveiled a dire threat to the team: contraction. The league was losing money, and the Twins were identified as one of its weakest moneymakers. When asked how the threat of elimination affected the Twins players, center fielder Torii Hunter said, "All you can do is get ready and prepare like you're going to have a season."

The Twins' legal obligation to play in the Metrodome in 2002 saved them from the chopping block, and the team played that season like it might be the last. New manager Ron Gardenhire, a bench coach for

CENTER FIELDER · KIRBY PUCKETT

What Kirby Puckett lacked in size, he made up for in passion for the game. The 5-foot-9 stick of dynamite played a spectacular center field, perfecting the art of leaping impossibly high above the fence to rob opponents of home runs (an art that another Minnesota center fielder, Torii Hunter, would later come to master as well). Puckett was the consummate teammate and positive clubhouse influence, playing each game with a joyful enthusiasm usually seen only in kids in the sandlot or city park. The whole baseball world mourned when he died of a stroke in 2006.

STATS

Twins seasons: 1984–95

Height: 5-foot-9

Weight: 220

- .318 career BA

- 6-time Gold Glove winner

- 10-time All-Star

- Baseball Hall of Fame inductee (2001)

KIRBY PUCKETT
CENTER FIELDER

MINNESOTA
TWINS

many years under Kelly, coached "small-ball"—a brand of baseball that involved winning games not with home runs but with timely bunts, shrewd base running, and tough defense.

Popular players such as Hunter, first baseman Doug Mientkiewicz, and third baseman Corey Koskie made nightly highlights with their award-winning defense, and pitchers Brad Radke and reliever Eddie Guardado made the most of limited run support with crafty hurling to catcher A. J. Pierzynski. Behind these players, Minnesota went 94–67 and won the AL Central to return to the playoffs.

In the 2002 AL Division Series (ALDS), the Twins pulled out a thrilling, three-games-to-two win over the Oakland A's. Pierzynski clouted a three-run, ninth-inning home run in Game 5 in Oakland to seal the series win and put the Twins in the ALCS versus the Anaheim Angels. The World Series remained beyond reach, though, as the Angels beat the Twins four games to one and went on to win the championship.

In both 2003 and 2004, with the threat of contraction behind them, the Twins repeated as division champs but were quickly subdued by the Yankees in the ALDS. Two new star pitchers emerged during those

TORII HUNTER

seasons: starter Johan Santana and closer Joe Nathan. Santana, a lefty from Venezuela with a blazing fastball and a nearly unhittable changeup, won the prestigious Cy Young Award as the AL's best pitcher in 2004.

The Twins put much of their hopes in young players in 2005, particularly catcher Joe Mauer and first baseman Justin Morneau. Mauer, who grew up in St. Paul, had an arm like a rifle and a sweet left-handed batting stroke. Morneau, meanwhile, was a strapping Canadian who could hit the ball a mile. Although the Twins missed the playoffs in 2005, more memorable baseball was coming.

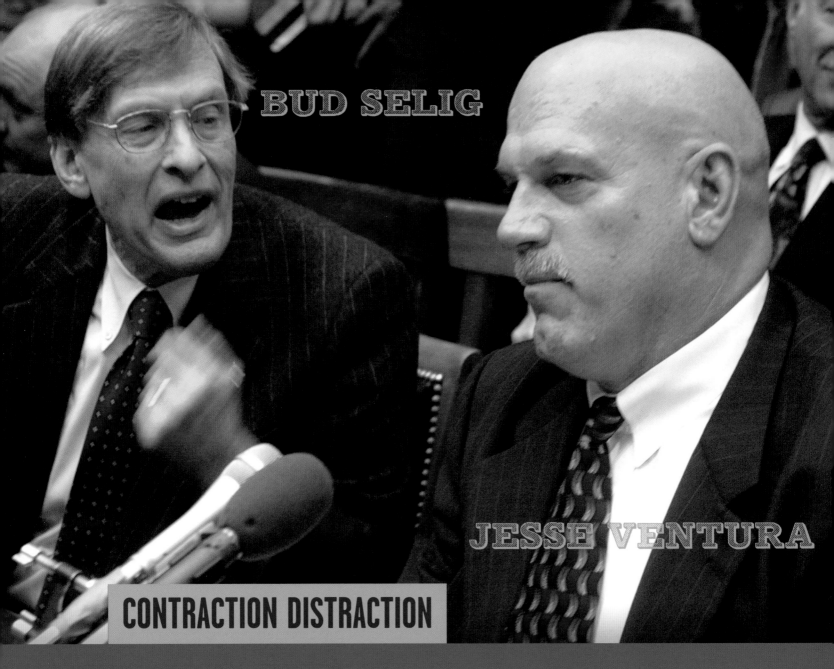

BUD SELIG

JESSE VENTURA

CONTRACTION DISTRACTION

In November 2001, Major League Baseball commissioner Bud Selig announced that 25 of baseball's 30 teams lost money during the 2001 season, leaving the league a large collective debt. At a meeting following the 2001 World Series, team owners voted 28–2 to contract, or eliminate, two teams. The leading candidates were two of the least profitable franchises, the Montreal Expos and the Minnesota Twins. The controversial issue was only one of baseball's problems at the time—the league had been losing fan support since a players' strike in 1994 had canceled that year's World Series. Some fans pointed to owners overpaying players as the reason for the lack of prosperity. "When a .250 hitter can sign a contract for $75 million, I think something is wrong at the top level of baseball that needs to be fixed," said Minnesota governor Jesse Ventura. In court, an injunction was upheld requiring the Twins to play in the Metrodome in 2002. And play the Twins did, winning the AL Central Division. The contraction threats died down as the Twins continued to win, and they faded into memory with the 2006 announcement that a new outdoor ballpark called Target Field would be built for the club in downtown Minneapolis by 2010.

TWINS

RIGHT FIELDER · TONY OLIVA

"Tony O" burst onto the major-league scene with a bang, winning the AL Rookie of the Year Award in 1964 and leading the league in batting average. A native of Cuba, Oliva hit for both power and average, and he played a sticky-fingered right field. Throughout the mid-to-late 1960s, Oliva teamed with Harmon Killebrew and Rod Carew to lead the Twins deep into the postseason. Bad knees cut short Oliva's career, which would certainly have been of Hall of Fame caliber had it lasted longer. In 1976, Oliva began a career as a coach and scout for the Twins organization, roles he still played as of 2010.

STATS

Twins seasons: 1962–76

Height: 6-foot-2

Weight: 190

- .304 career BA

- 947 career RBI

- 8-time All-Star

- Uniform number (6) retired by Twins

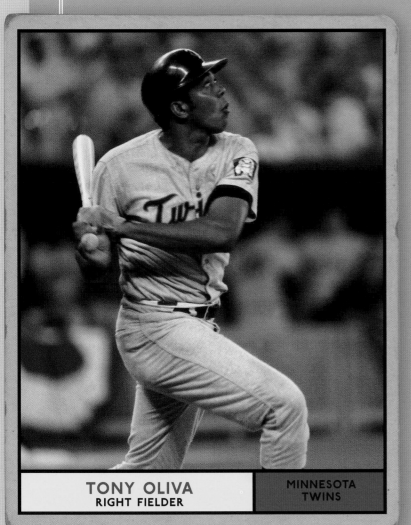

TONY OLIVA
RIGHT FIELDER

MINNESOTA
TWINS

MANAGER · TOM KELLY

"T.K." was to the Minnesota Twins what a hot cup of coffee is to a sleepy person in the morning—a sobering, straightforward wake-up call. In 1986, Kelly was named Minnesota's manager when he was just 36, but what he lacked in experience he made up for with a no-nonsense approach to teaching. He encouraged his players to play baseball the right way—with hustle, heart, and an allegiance to the fundamentals of the game. Prior to managing, the Minnesota native played 49 games for the Twins as a first baseman in 1975, hitting 1 home run.

STATS

Twins seasons as manager: 1986– 2001

Managerial record: 1,140–1,244

World Series championships: 1987, 1991

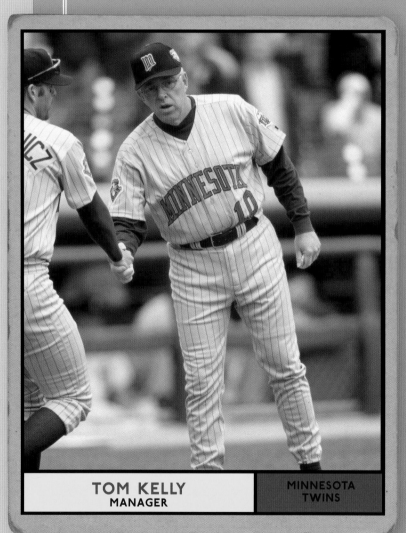

TOM KELLY
MANAGER

MINNESOTA
TWINS

FANTASTIC FINISHES

n 2006, the Twins' record stood at 25–33 on June 7. But then the ballclub dropped some slumping veterans from the roster, giving more playing time to energetic youngsters such as shortstop Jason Bartlett. Utilizing a lineup that once again played small-ball, the Twins proceeded to win 21 of their next 23 games, stayed hot, and eventually overtook the Tigers to win the division on the final day of the season.

The celebratory atmosphere in Minnesota ended quickly, as the Twins were swept by the A's in the ALDS. Still, Minnesota's list of player accomplishments in 2006 was long: Santana won his second Cy Young Award; rookie pitcher Francisco Liriano earned All-Star status with a 12–3 record before suffering an elbow injury; Mauer hit his way to the AL batting title; and Morneau broke through as a star by blasting 34 homers with 130 runs batted in (RBI) to win the AL MVP award.

Although the Twins fell short of the postseason in 2007, wins and losses became something of an afterthought when the Interstate 35W Mississippi River Bridge, located mere blocks from the Metrodome, collapsed before a Twins game on August 1. The disaster cost 13 people their lives and left more than 100 others injured. A moment of silence was observed before the start of that day's game and before all home games the rest of the season.

Financially unable to pay superstar-level salaries, Minnesota was forced to trade away Santana after the 2007 season and watch Hunter leave town for a richer contract elsewhere. Still, the team's 2008 hopes were buoyed by a young, promising pitching staff that included Scott Baker and Nick Blackburn. Minnesota also fielded an impressive lineup with such players as Mauer, Morneau, and outfielders Denard Span and Michael Cuddyer. By the end of the 2008 season, the Twins and the Chicago White Sox were tied with identical 88–74 records. In a one-game playoff to decide the division championship, the Twins got a superb pitching performance from Blackburn but lost an agonizing 1–0 decision in Chicago.

Minnesota, amazingly, again found itself tied for AL Central honors at the end of the 2009 season and again went to a 163rd game to break the tie, this time against the Tigers. The game was played in the Metrodome, which was serving out the end of its 28-season tenure as the home of

THE PIRANHAS

The Twins' 2006 season was remarkable on many levels, and one of the main reasons was the "Piranhas." After playing the first two months of the season with a number of overpaid veterans and racking up a disappointing 27–34 record, the Twins decided to let some of the veterans go and play a more youthful lineup. Shortstop Jason Bartlett and outfielder Jason Tyner were called up from the minors, teaming with infielders Nick Punto and Luis Castillo to occupy the first, second, eighth, and ninth spots in the Twins' batting order. Although none of them added much power to the lineup, all four were scrappy, speedy players who were good at hitting singles and bunting, and the change effectively gave the Twins four leadoff batters in a row. After these players helped the Twins down the Chicago White Sox in an August series, Chicago manager Ozzie Guillen gave the players a nickname they would proudly embrace. "All those piranhas—blooper here, blooper here, beat out a ground ball, hit a home run, they're up by four," said Guillen, alluding to the small but famously fierce fish of South America. "They get up by four with that bullpen? See you at the national anthem tomorrow."

TWINS

Star catcher and reigning AL MVP Joe Mauer helped break in Target Field in 2010 after signing an 8-year, $184-million contract with his hometown team.

JOE MAUER

Francisco Liriano (above) and Delmon Young (opposite) both pulled their weight in 2010; Liriano won 14 games, while Young drove in 112 runs.

DELMON YOUNG

the Twins. With the Dome rocking, the Twins and Tigers played an incredible, back-and-forth game that saw Minnesota finally secure a 6–5 victory in 12 innings.

Although the Yankees continued their postseason dominance over the Twins, swiftly sweeping Minnesota out of the playoffs, Minnesota fans had reason to celebrate both the season and their favorite homegrown hero. Mauer became the fifth AL MVP in Twins history, winning the 2009 award after clinching his third AL batting title with a sizzling .365 average and 28 home runs. Mauer and his teammates, including veteran slugger Jim Thome, christened their new park, Target Field, with another division crown in 2010. Unfortunately, Minnesota's playoff woes continued as it was then swept yet again by New York. "We haven't got it done," lamented Gardenhire. "You just have to put it together at the right time."

The Minnesota Twins' history is a colorful one that involves one relocation, two world championships, prolonged slumps, some all-time greats, decades of playing under a Teflon roof, and now, baseball back under the summer sun. If today's Twins catch a break or two and realize their full potential, Minnesota may soon be decorating its new ballpark with championship banners.

INDEX